NORTH AMERICAN MAMMALS

Mountain Lion

Jinny Johnson

Published by Smart Apple Media,
an imprint of Black Rabbit Books
P.O. Box 3263, Mankato, Minnesota, 56002
www.blackrabbitbooks.com

Printed in the United States of America,
at Corporate Graphics in North Mankato, Minnesota.

Designed by Hel James
Edited by Mary-Jane Wilkins

Cataloging-in-Publication Data
is available from the Library of Congress

ISBN 978-1-62588-035-2

Photo acknowledgements
t = top, b = bottom
title page creativex/Shutterstock; page 3 visceralimage/
Shutterstock; 4 Tom Brakefield/Thinkstock; 5 Dennis Donohue/
Shutterstock; 6 Stockphoto/Thinkstock; 7 Dennis Donohue/
Shutterstock; 8 Stockphoto/Thinkstock; 9 Scott E Read/
Shutterstock; 10 worldswildlifewonders/Shutterstock;
11 NancyS/Shutterstock; 12 Tom Brakefield/Thinkstock;
14 creativex/Shutterstock; 15 Tom Brakefield/Thinkstock;
16, 17 Hemera/Thinkstock; 18, 19 iStockphoto/Thinkstock;
20 outdoorsman/Shutterstock; 21 iStockphoto/Thinkstock;
22t Hemera/Thinkstock, b Pavel K/Shutterstock; 23 Tony Rix/
Shutterstock
Cover NancyS/Shutterstock

DAD0509
052013
9 8 7 6 5 4 3 2 1

Contents

I'm a mountain lion.

I have lots of other names too, such as cougar, puma, and panther. They're all me.

My Home

I'm happy to make my home anywhere, from forests and mountains to deserts, but I do like to have lots of space to roam around.

I'm a loner.
I prefer to live
and hunt by
myself—except
when I have
kittens, of course.

Golden Lion

Look at me. I'm big and strong
with a long tail that helps me balance
when I'm running and jumping.

My paws are large and
I have sharp claws and
teeth for attacking prey.

My golden color helps me stay hidden among rocks and bushes as I track prey. I do have little black marks on the back of my ears though, and a black tip on my tail.

Running and Jumping

My long back legs help me run and jump. I can race along at up to 50 miles an hour (80 km/h) for a short time and make huge leaps along the way.

I can also jump as much as 15 feet (4.5 m) up into a tree or onto a rock—that's more than twice as high as an adult person.

I'm a good climber and I even swim when I have to.

Night Hunter

I often take it easy during the day and go out in the late afternoon to start looking for food. I'm busiest from dusk, when darkness falls, until the early morning.

I have great hearing and I can see well in low light, which is important when I go hunting at night. My sense of smell is pretty good too.

Favorite Foods

I'm a hunter and I only eat meat.

Deer are my favorite food, but I'll gobble up anything I can catch, such as rabbits, hares, and skunks. I'll even tackle a spiky porcupine.

If I kill a large animal I drag
it to a hiding place and
feed on it for several days.

Hunting

When I hunt I usually sneak up on the prey, keeping as quiet as I possibly can.

When I'm as close as I can get, I make a speedy pounce and kill my victim with a bite to the neck.

I'm not always lucky though. Sometimes the prey animal escapes and I have to start all over again.

Sounds and Smells

Mountain lions don't roar, but we do purr and make chirruping sounds.

We also sometimes make loud screaming calls, which people find scary.

We use smell to send messages too. I mark my home range with scratches on tree trunks and with pee and poop. This tells other mountain lions that this is my area.

17

My Family

 Earlier this year I had my first kittens.

I gave birth to them in my den inside a cave and I fed them with my milk. When they were a few months old I let them come out of the den to play.

They were still very tiny, so I watched them carefully and didn't let them go far from me.

Growing Up

Now my kittens are six months old and they come with me when I go hunting.

They stay out of sight and keep very quiet while they watch what I do.

They will stay with me until they have learned all they need to know about hunting and living by themselves.

When they are about three years old I hope they will have families of their own.

Mountain Lion Facts

Mountain lions belong to the cat family of mammals. They are the biggest cats in North America. They live in western North America and in South America.

A full-grown animal is about 4 feet (1.2 m) long, with a tail measuring another 27 inches (69 cm) or so. An average male mountain lion weighs about 135 pounds (61 kg). Females are smaller and lighter.

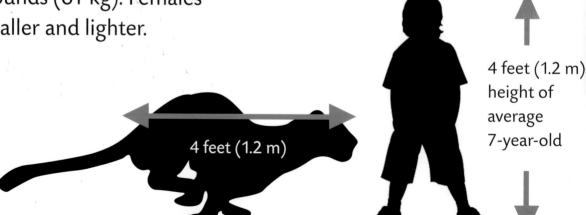

4 feet (1.2 m)

4 feet (1.2 m) height of average 7-year-old

These cats are champion jumpers and the record jump for a mountain lion on level ground is more than 38 feet (11.5 m)— even Olympic athletes can only jump just over 29 feet (nearly 9 m).

Once there were many more mountain lions and they lived over most of North America. Many have been hunted and shot because they sometimes prey on farm animals.

Useful Words

dusk The time of the evening just before it gets dark.

prey Animals caught and killed by animals such as mountain lions.

Index

claws 6
climbing 9
color 7

den 19

food 10, 12, 13

hearing 11
hunting 5, 10, 11, 12, 14, 15, 20, 21

jumping 6, 8, 9, 23

kittens 5, 18, 19, 20, 21

prey 6, 7, 12, 13, 14, 15, 23, 24

smell 11, 17
sounds 17
swimming 9

tail 6, 7, 22

Web Link

Learn more about mountain lions at
www.sandiegozoo.org/animalbytes/t-puma.html